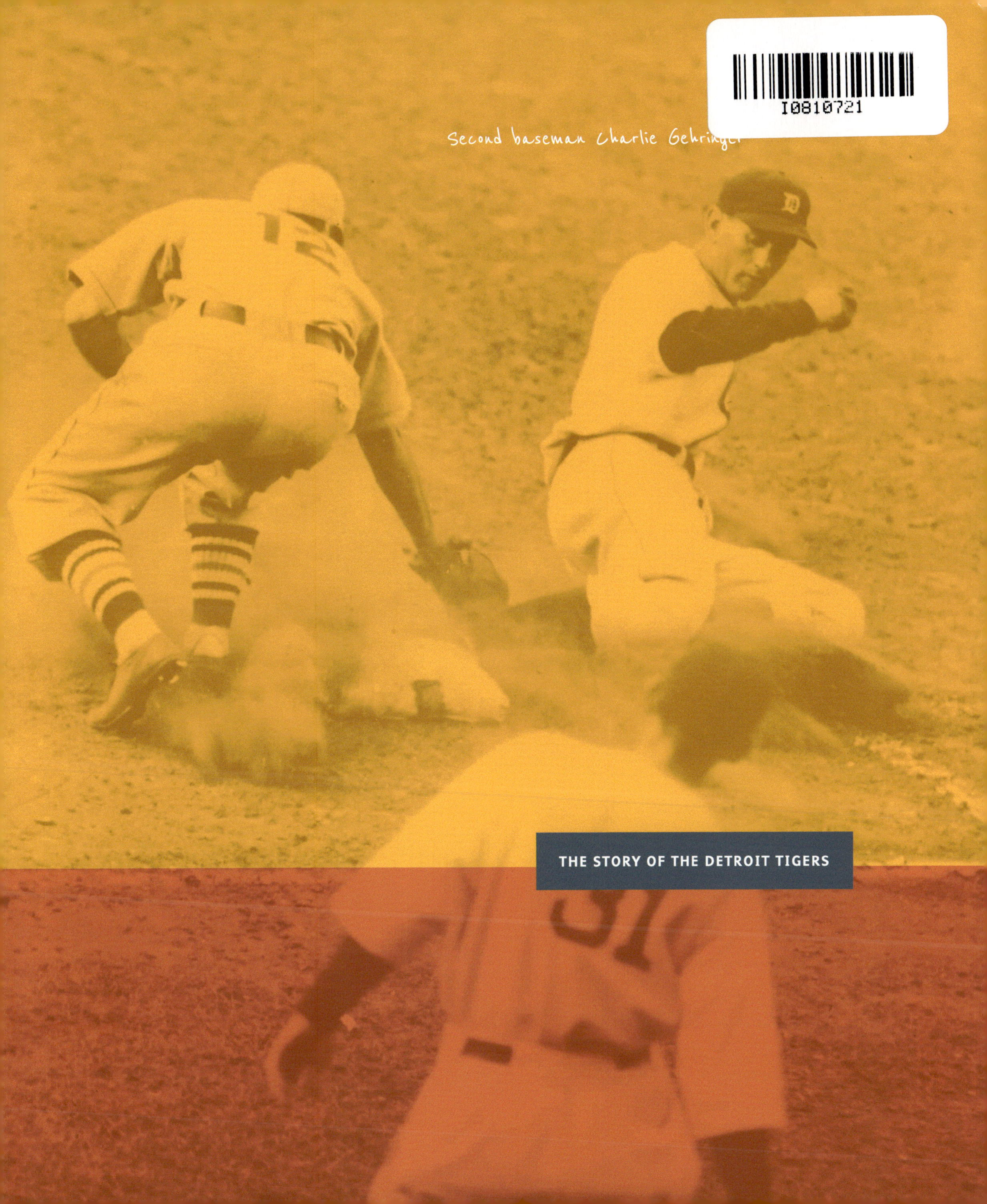

Second baseman Charlie Gehringer

THE STORY OF THE DETROIT TIGERS

Shortstop Javier Báez

THE STORY OF THE

DETROIT TIGERS

JOE TISCHLER

CREATIVE SPORTS

Pitcher Justin Verlander

CREATIVE EDUCATION / CREATIVE PAPERBACKS

Published by Creative Education and Creative Paperbacks
P.O. Box 227, Mankato, Minnesota 56002
Creative Education and Creative Paperbacks are imprints of The Creative Company
www.thecreativecompany.us

Book Design by Graham Morgan
Art direction by Blue Design (www.bluedes.com)

Images by Alamy Stock Photo/ZUMA, 29; Getty Images/B Bennett, 9, Focus On Sport, 7 (top, left), 7 (bottom, right), 10, 11, FPG, 1, George Kubas/Diamond Images, 2, Gregory Shamus, 6 (bottom, right), Mark Rucker/Transcendental Graphics, 4–5, 32, MLB Photos, 20, National Baseball Hall of Fame Library, 6 (bottom, left), 19, Nick Cammett/Diamond Images, cover, 30, 31, Patrick McDermott, 3, Photo File/MLB, cover, 18, Pictorial Parade, 7 (top, right), Rich Pilling, 7 (bottom, left), 22–23, 25, Ron Vesely, 6 (top, left), Stephen Green, 26-27; Library of Congress/Bain News Service, publisher, 15; Public Domain/Charles M. Conlon, 12; Wikimedia Commons/Louis Van Oeyen, 6 (top, right), public domain, 10, The Sporting News Archives/public domain, 16

Library of Congress Cataloging-in-Publication Data
Names: Tischler, Joe author
Title: The story of the Detroit Tigers / by Joe Tischler.
Description: Mankato, Minnesota : Creative Education and Creative Paperbacks, [2026] | Series: Creative sports. Major League baseball | Includes index. | Audience: Ages 8-12 | Audience: Grades 4-6 | Summary: "Discover the Detroit Tigers' thrilling journey from early triumphs and World Series wins to recent victories, featuring legendary players and the Major League Baseball team's dedicated fanbase. Written for middle-grade readers. Includes table of contents, sidebars, and index"—Provided by publisher.
Identifiers: LCCN 2025020674 (print) | LCCN 2025020675 (ebook) | ISBN 9798895810934 library binding | ISBN 9798896800460 paperback | ISBN 9798895812198 ebook
Subjects: LCSH: Detroit Tigers (Baseball team)—History—Juvenile literature | World Series (Baseball)—History—Juvenile literature | Baseball—Michigan—Detroit—History, Local—Juvenile literature
Classification: LCC GV875.D6 T575 2026 (print) | LCC GV875.D6 (ebook) | DDC 796.357/640977434—dc23/eng/20250626
LC record available at https://lccn.loc.gov/2025020674
LC ebook record available at https://lccn.loc.gov/2025020675

Printed in the United States

Right fielder Harry Heilmann

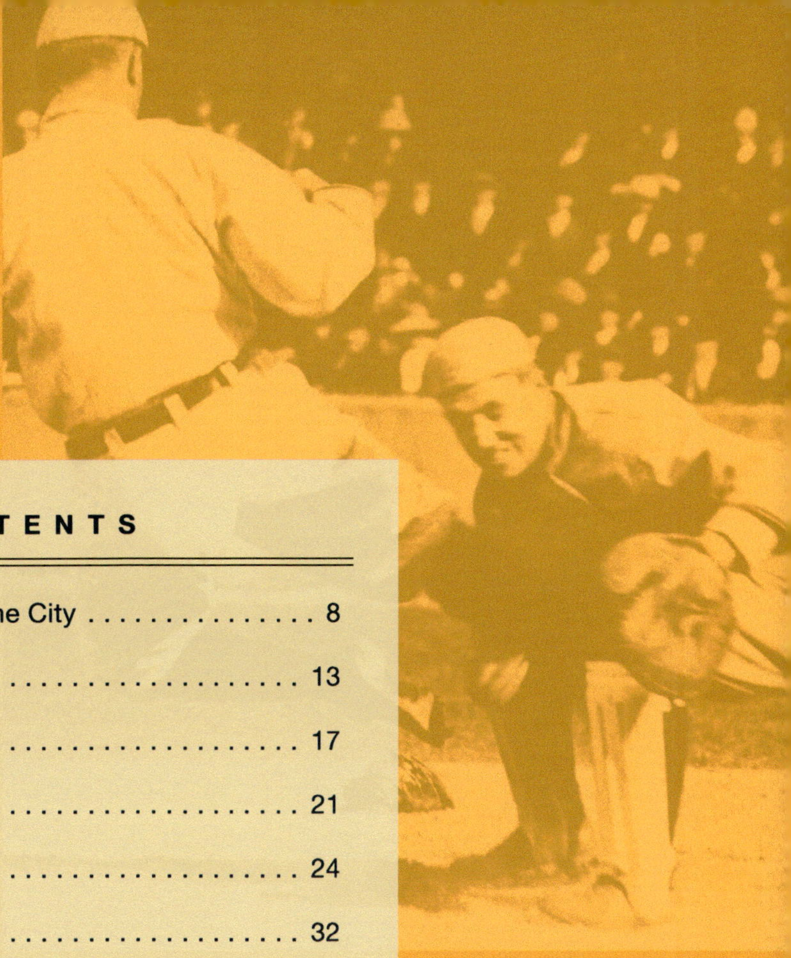

CONTENTS

EXTRA INNINGS

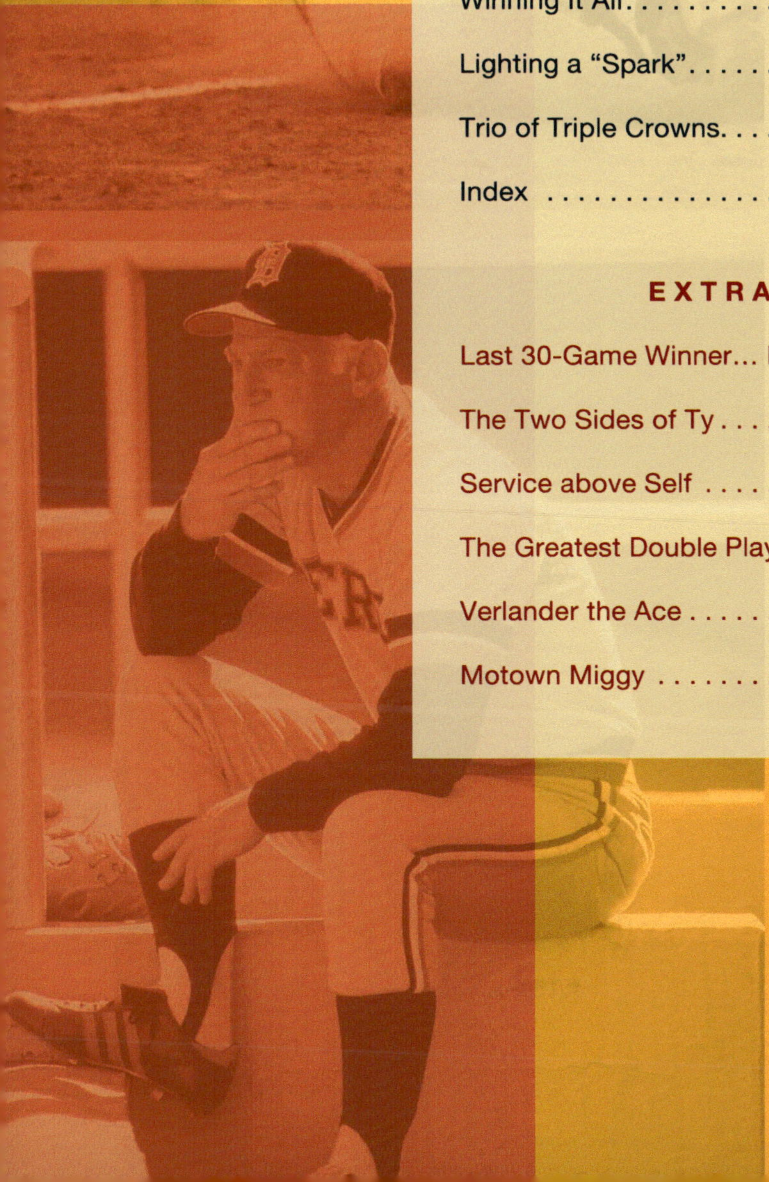

WORLD CHAMPIONSHIP FOR THE CITY

The summer of 1967 was tough for the city of Detroit, Michigan. One of the worst urban riots in American history took place in the city. It began on Sunday, July 23. The Detroit Tigers hosted a Major League Baseball (MLB) doubleheader that day. Fans leaving were asked to avoid certain areas of the city. The riots lasted five days. The Tigers were forced to postpone home games. Forty-three people died. Nearly 1,200 people were injured. More than 400 buildings were destroyed.

Through it all, the Tigers were in a tight pennant race in 1967. They were battling the Boston Red Sox and Minnesota Twins for the top spot in the American League (AL). Going into the final day of the season, Detroit trailed Minnesota and Boston by one-half game. The Red Sox and Twins played each other in Boston. The Tigers played a home doubleheader against the California Angels. Detroit won the opening game to move into a three-way tie. Boston beat Minnesota. But the Tigers lost the second game of the doubleheader. Boston won the pennant.

Pitcher Denny McLain

EXTRA INNINGS

DENNY MCLAIN
PITCHER
TIGERS SEASONS: 1963–70
HEIGHT: 6-FOOT-1
WEIGHT: 185 POUNDS
KEY STATS: 1968 AL MVP, 2X AL CY YOUNG WINNER, 3X ALL-STAR, 1968 WORLD SERIES CHAMPION

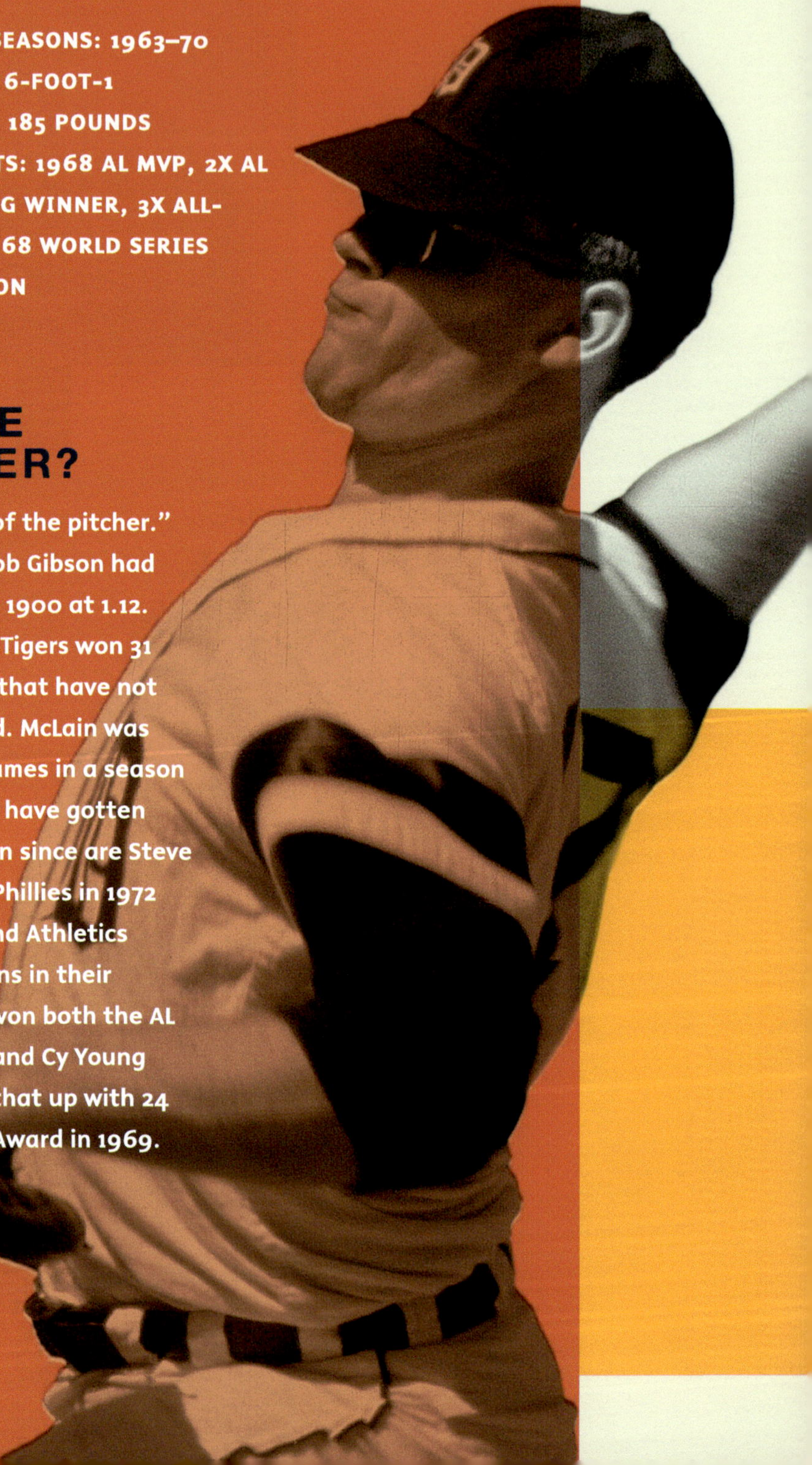

LAST 30-GAME WINNER... EVER?

1968 is known as "the year of the pitcher." St. Louis Cardinals pitcher Bob Gibson had the second-lowest ERA since 1900 at 1.12. Denny McLain of the Detroit Tigers won 31 games. Those are two feats that have not come close to being matched. McLain was the first pitcher to win 30 games in a season since 1934. The pitchers who have gotten closest to 30 wins in a season since are Steve Carlton of the Philadelphia Phillies in 1972 and Bob Welch of the Oakland Athletics in 1990. Both recorded 27 wins in their respective seasons. McLain won both the AL Most Valuable Player (MVP) and Cy Young Award in 1968. He followed that up with 24 wins and another Cy Young Award in 1969.

First baseman Norm Cash, 1968 World Series

There was no late-season drama for the 1968 Tigers. They grabbed first place in the AL on May 10. Their lead only grew from there. Detroit won 103 games. It won the pennant by 12 games. The team was led on the mound by Denny McLain. He won 31 games that year. No MLB pitcher since has won at least 30 games in a season.

Detroit played the St. Louis Cardinals in the World Series. The Cardinals had won the World Series the previous season. They had an equally impressive pitcher. Bob Gibson had a minuscule earned run average (ERA) of 1.12. That is the third-lowest ERA in National League (NL) history.

McLain had a tough start to the World Series. He pitched against Gibson in Games 1 and 4. The Cardinals easily won both games. They held a 3–1 series lead. Detroit needed to find an edge to stay alive in the series in Game 5. It came from starting pitcher Mickey Lolich. He recorded the Tigers' lone win in the series with an 8–1 score in Game 2. Lolich was on the mound for Game 5. He gave up three first inning runs. But he held St. Louis scoreless the rest of the game. Al Kaline drove in two runs in the seventh inning that gave Detroit the lead. The Tigers won 5–3.

McLain was on the mound for Game 6. He went all nine innings, allowing only one run. Detroit's bats made a statement. The Tigers scored 10 times in the third inning. Detroit won 13–1. The series was tied at three games apiece.

Detroit called on Lolich for Game 7. St. Louis countered with Gibson. The game was scoreless going into the seventh inning. The Tigers finally broke through. Jim Northrup's triple scored two. Detroit scored three times in the inning. It was more than enough for Lolich. He recorded his third win of the series. Detroit won 4–1. The Tigers were world champions! It was just what the city of Detroit needed following the turbulent summer of 1967.

THE HITTING MACHINE

The Detroit franchise began in 1894. It played in a minor league called the Western League. Officials looked to history for a team name. During the Civil War, a Michigan army unit was called the Detroit Light Guard. The soldiers were known for their fierce fighting. They were nicknamed the Tigers. The Detroit baseball team received permission from the Light Guard to use the Tigers nickname.

In 1900, the Western League was renamed the American League. The following year, it became a major league. The Tigers finished with a winning record in their first major-league season. Three straight losing seasons followed. They achieved a 79–74 mark in 1905. That year, Detroit's lineup included scrappy rookie center fielder Ty Cobb. The 18-year-old batted just .238. It would be the only season in his 24-year career that he did not top .300. He hit above .400 three times. Fellow outfielder Sam Crawford disliked

Center fielder Ty Cobb

Cobb intensely. Yet the duo played well together. Crawford called Cobb "the best player I've ever seen."

Cobb captured his first AL batting title in 1907. He led Detroit to their first AL pennant. The team faced the Chicago Cubs in the World Series. The Tigers were swept. They lost to the Cubs again in the World Series the following season. Detroit returned a third time to the World Series in 1909. The Pittsburgh Pirates beat them in seven games.

Detroit had a series of up-and-down seasons after that. The 1915 season was particularly frustrating. Cobb won his ninth-straight batting title. He drove in 99 runs and stole 96 bases. The Tigers won 100 games. But the Boston Red Sox won 101. Detroit was out of the playoffs.

By 1921, the Tigers added another star. Outfielder Harry Heilmann batted .394. He edged out Cobb for the batting title. Detroit continued to produce strong swingers. But it spent most of the 1920s hovering near the middle of the standings.

Things were not much better in the early 1930s. Detroit soon added veteran star catcher Mickey Cochrane. He also managed the team. Slugger Hank Greenberg covered first base. Charlie Gehringer was nearly flawless at second. The Tigers won a franchise-best 101 games in 1934. They won the pennant for the first time in 25 years. Detroit took a three-games-to-two lead against the St. Louis Cardinals in the World Series. But Detroit dropped the final two games at home, including an 11–0 loss in Game 7.

Detroit returned to the World Series in 1935. It faced the Cubs. The Tigers had a chance to clinch the series again on their home field. This time, they were successful. Goose Goslin hit the game-winning single in the bottom of the ninth of Game 6. Detroit won 4 games to 2. The Tigers were finally world champions! "I've had many big moments in my life," said Cochrane. "But none to equal the thrill of crossing the plate with the winning run."

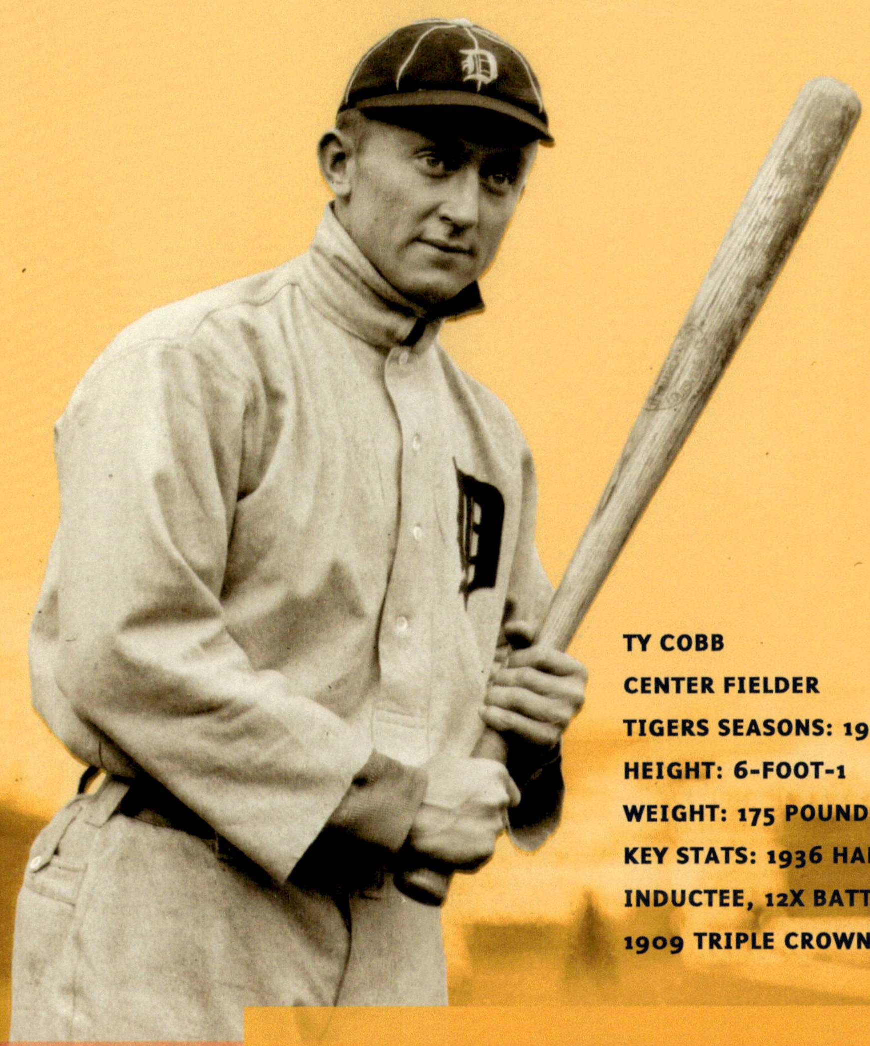

EXTRA INNINGS

TY COBB
CENTER FIELDER
TIGERS SEASONS: 1905–26
HEIGHT: 6-FOOT-1
WEIGHT: 175 POUNDS
KEY STATS: 1936 HALL OF FAME INDUCTEE, 12X BATTING TITLE, 1909 TRIPLE CROWN, 1911 AL MVP

THE TWO SIDES OF TY

Born and raised in Georgia, Ty Cobb was nicknamed "The Georgia Peach." He won the AL batting title 12 times. His lifetime batting average was .366. That is still a major-league record. Cobb was also a daring base stealer. He stole second, third, and home in the same inning four different times. He stole 96 bases in 1915 alone. His career total was 897. Both were modern major-league records that stood for nearly 50 years. Cobb was also one of the most disliked players in MLB history. He had a hostile temper. Still, fellow players respected his undeniable talent.

EXTRA INNINGS

HANK GREENBERG
FIRST BASEMAN AND LEFT FIELDER
TIGERS SEASONS:
1930, 1933–41, 1945–46
HEIGHT: 6-FOOT-3
WEIGHT: 210 POUNDS
KEY STATS: 1956 HALL OF FAME INDUCTEE, 2X AL MVP, 4X ALL-STAR, 4X AL HOME RUN LEADER

SERVICE ABOVE SELF

"Hammerin' Hank" Greenberg topped the AL in home runs three times from 1935 to 1940. He was drafted into the U.S. Army in 1941. He missed most of that season. Greenberg was honorably discharged on December 5. Two days later, the Japanese attacked U.S. military bases in Hawaii. Greenberg joined the Army Air Force. "We are in trouble," he said, "and there is only one thing for me to do—return to service. This doubtless means I am finished with baseball." But when World War II ended in 1945, Greenberg rejoined the Tigers. The following year, he led the major league in home runs.

WINNING IT ALL

The Tigers continued to compile winning records. In 1940, Detroit won the AL pennant by a single game over the Cleveland Indians. Pitcher Bobo Newsom had 21 wins. Detroit met the Cincinnati Reds in the World Series. The Tigers took a three-games-to-two lead in the series. The Reds won Game 6, setting up a decisive Game 7. Newsom took the mound on just a day's rest. Detroit led 1–0 in the seventh inning. But the Reds scored twice in the inning to take the lead. The Tigers could not score in the final two innings. Cincinnati won the series.

In 1944, pitcher Hal Newhouser notched 29 wins. He was named AL Most Valuable Player (MVP). Fellow hurler Dizzy Trout added 27 more. He was second in MVP voting. Detroit finished behind the St. Louis Browns by just one game for the AL pennant. Newhouser repeated as MVP the following season. He is the only pitcher to win MVP in consecutive seasons. Hank Greenberg returned following three years of service during World War II. He gave the team a boost. The Tigers faced the Cubs in the World Series. In the deciding Game 7, Chicago cycled through six pitchers. Newhouser pitched a complete game. The Tigers won, 9–3.

Detroit enjoyed winning records for the rest of the 1940s. But it posted a franchise-worst 50–104 record in 1952. The team signed a promising rookie to help it out of its slump. Al Kaline was a slender, 18-year-old right fielder. He struggled at the plate in his first year. Ted Williams advised him to strengthen his wrists. So Kaline squeezed baseballs as hard as he could. He swung weighted bats. Such off-season training seemed to pay off. He hit .340 in

Right fielder Al Kaline

1955. Now 20, he became the youngest player to win the league batting title. Williams said, "There's no telling how far the kid could go."

Despite the talents of Kaline and shortstop Harvey Kuenn, Detroit struggled for the rest of the 1950s. From 1960 to 1961, the Tigers had a remarkable 30-game improvement. Unfortunately, they finished eight games behind the Yankees in the American League. The team put together winning seasons in five of the next six years. The 1967 team lost out on its chance to win the pennant on the last day of the season.

The Tigers broke through in 1968. They won 103 games and topped St. Louis in the World Series. Denny McLain won 31 games. He took home both the AL MVP and Cy Young awards. Fellow pitcher Mickey Lolich went 3–0 in the World Series, throwing three complete games. He was named series MVP.

The following year, the league split into two divisions. Detroit won 90 games in the AL East Division. But the Baltimore Orioles topped the division with an astounding 109 wins.

Three years later, Detroit won the division for the first time. It faced the Oakland Athletics in the AL Championship Series (ALCS). The Tigers lost the first two games. They bounced back to win the next two. But Oakland won Game 5 to take the best-of-five series.

Pitcher Hal Newhouser

EXTRA INNINGS

ALAN TRAMMELL (PICTURED)
SHORTSTOP
TIGERS SEASONS: 1977–96
HEIGHT: 6-FOOT
WEIGHT: 175 POUNDS
KEY STATS: 2018 HALL OF FAME INDUCTEE, 6X ALL-STAR, 4X GOLD GLOVE, 1984 WORLD SERIES MVP

LOU WHITAKER
SECOND BASEMAN
TIGERS SEASONS: 1977–95
HEIGHT: 5-FOOT-11
WEIGHT: 160 POUNDS
KEY STATS: 1978 AL ROOKIE OF THE YEAR, 5X ALL-STAR, 3X GOLD GLOVE, 4X SILVER SLUGGER

THE GREATEST DOUBLE PLAY COMBO EVER

A team's shortstop and second baseman are considered "double-play combinations." These are the positions most involved in double plays. In 1977, The Tigers started the longest-tenured and perhaps best double-play combination of all time. They were destined to be paired together. Alan Trammell and Lou Whitaker made their big-league debuts with Detroit on the same day. They got their first big-league hits in the same game against the same pitcher. They were teammates for 19 years. Together they turned more than 1,100 double plays together. That is a major-league record. Combined, they won seven Gold Glove awards. The two were good with the bat, too. Together, they won a total of seven Silver Slugger awards.

LIGHTING A "SPARK"

The Tigers struggled for several seasons. They posted a woeful 57–102 record in 1975. Detroit signed rookie Mark Fidrych before the 1976 season. The lanky pitcher was nicknamed "The Bird." He created a league-wide sensation. The Bird led the majors with a 2.34 earned run average (ERA). He was named Rookie of the Year. But the Tigers could muster only a 74–87 finish.

Midway through the 1979 season, Detroit hired Sparky Anderson as manager. He had led Cincinnati to two world championships. He boldly predicted the Tigers would win the pennant within five years. Each year, his players progressed toward that goal. Catcher Lance Parrish began perfecting his home run swing. Outfielder Kirk Gibson became a consistent hitter. Slick-fielding shortstop Alan Trammell and second baseman Lou Whitaker developed into one of the best double-play duos in the majors. Fiery pitcher Jack Morris won 20 games in 1983. But the team finished six games behind the Orioles.

In 1984, the Tigers started the season winning an amazing 35 of their first 40 games. They roared to 104 wins. They finished 15 games ahead of the Toronto Blue Jays in the division. It was exactly five years after Anderson's prediction. The Tigers swept the Kansas City Royals in the ALCS. They faced the San Diego Padres in the World Series. Detroit defeated the Padres in five games. An emotional Anderson told his players, "Don't forget this moment. You did it all."

In 1987, Detroit and Toronto were neck-and-neck for the AL East division title. The Blue Jays led the division by one game over Detroit with three games left in the season. The Tigers hosted Toronto for the final series. Detroit won

The Detroit Tigers celebrate on the field after winning the 1984 World Series.

all three games. It returned to the postseason. But the Minnesota Twins knocked them out in five games. The Tigers nearly returned to the playoffs the following season. But they finished one game behind the Boston Red Sox for the division title.

Detroit dropped to last place in 1989. The team added big first baseman Cecil Fielder. He hit 51 home runs in 1990. The next year, he slammed 44. He also piled up 113 runs batted in (RBI) in 1991. The Tigers tied for second in the AL East. But they stumbled the next few years. Anderson left after the 1995 season. Gibson and Whitaker retired. Trammell followed suit the next year. Detroit finished 53–109 that season. It was the most losses in team history.

The team joined the newly formed AL Central Division in 1998. It finished last. In 1999, the Tigers played their final season in Tiger Stadium. A crowd of 43,356 fans turned out for the last home game. The team opened their new stadium, Comerica Park in 2000. It finished 79–83 in their new home.

After two poor seasons, the Tigers hired longtime fan favorite Alan Trammell as manager in 2003. They lost 119 games. That set an American League record for most losses in a season.

TRIO OF TRIPLE CROWNS

Detroit made a surprise free-agent acquisition before the 2004 season. Catcher Iván Rodríguez joined the team. He was a 10-time All-Star and 10-time Gold Glove winner. He helped the Tigers to a 29-win improvement from the previous season. By 2006, the rebuilt Tigers were World Series contenders. They won 95 games and clinched a Wild Card

Catcher Iván Rodríguez

Wilson

JUSTIN VERLANDER
PITCHER
TIGERS SEASONS: 2005–17
HEIGHT: 6-FOOT-5
WEIGHT: 240 POUNDS
KEY STATS: 2006 AL ROOKIE OF THE YEAR, 3X CY YOUNG, 2011 TRIPLE CROWN, 5X STRIKEOUT LEADER

EXTRA INNINGS

VERLANDER THE ACE

Detroit lost 119 games in 2003. That allowed them to have a high pick in the 2004 MLB Draft. They picked Justin Verlander with the second overall selection. It was a great pick. Verlander's first full season was 2006. He won 17 games and was the AL Rookie of the Year. He had one of the best seasons ever for a pitcher in 2011. He won the pitching triple crown and both the AL Cy Young and AL MVP awards. He later went on to pitch for the Houston Astros, New York Mets, and San Francisco Giants. He is one of only two pitchers ever to win a World Series title, an MVP, a Rookie of the Year award, and a Cy Young.

berth. Pitcher Justin Verlander stormed onto the scene. He won 17 games and was named AL Rookie of the Year. Detroit knocked off the Yankees in the AL Division Series (ALDS). Then they swept Oakland in the ALCS. The Tigers faced St. Louis in the World Series. The teams split the first two games. But the Cardinals won the next three to win the series.

Verlander continued to thrill fans in 2007. He tossed his first career no-hitter. Detroit made another stellar acquisition in 2008. Prior to the season, it traded for Miguel Cabrera. In his first season in Detroit, he led the AL in home runs with 37. But the Tigers fell short of the playoffs. They were back in contention in 2009. Detroit held a seven-game division lead in early September. But the Tigers slipped down the stretch while the Twins got hot. The two teams tied for the division lead. A one game tiebreaker was needed. It was played in Minnesota. The Twins won in 12 innings.

By 2011, Verlander was the game's premier pitcher. He won the Triple Crown of pitching. Verlander led the AL with 24 wins and a 2.40 ERA. He also recorded 250 strikeouts. The Tigers cruised to a division title. They defeated the Yankees again in the ALDS. But they fell to the Texas Rangers in the ALCS. The Tigers had another Triple Crown winner the following season. On the offensive side, Cabrera led the AL in batting average (.330), home runs (44), and runs batted in (139). Detroit was back in the playoffs. It topped the Athletics and Yankees in the AL playoffs. But they were swept in the World Series by the San Francisco Giants.

The Tigers came back strong in 2013. They won their division for the third year in a row. Detroit found another pitching ace in Max Scherzer. He won the Cy Young Award in 2013 after posting 21 wins. They knocked off Oakland again in the ALDS. But Boston topped them in the ALCS in six games. A fourth straight division title followed in 2014. But the Baltimore Orioles swept them out of the playoffs.

The Tigers fell on hard times following 2014. They had only one winning record over the next nine seasons. The low point came in 2019. They lost 114

EXTRA INNINGS

MIGUEL CABRERA
FIRST BASEMAN AND THIRD BASEMAN
TIGERS SEASONS: 2008–23
HEIGHT: 6–4
WEIGHT: 267 POUNDS
KEY STATS: 2X MVP, 2012 TRIPLE CROWN, 12X ALL-STAR, 4X BATTING TITLE

MOTOWN MIGGY

The Tigers pulled off one of the best trades in franchise history before the 2008 season. Miguel Cabrera came over from the Florida Marlins. It was the beginning of 16 great years with the franchise. He led the AL in home runs his first season. In 2009, he started a string of eight-straight .300 seasons. Four of those seasons resulted in batting titles. In 2012, he won the batting triple crown. He led the AL with 44 home runs, 139 RBI, and a .330 batting average. He won back-to-back AL MVP awards in 2012 and 2013. During his career, Cabrera hit 511 home runs and drove in 1,881 runs.

meijer
Detroit
31

Pitcher Tarik Skubal

games. Detroit gradually improved their winning percentage over the next four seasons. In the COVID-shortened 2020 season, the Tigers went 23–35. By 2023, they improved to 78 wins, just under .500.

The first half of the 2024 season seemed to follow the pattern of the previous nine seasons. In early July, the club sat nine games below .500. On August 10, they were still eight games below .500. Then, they went on a tear. The Tigers finished the season 31–13. They won 86 games and qualified for the playoffs as a Wild Card team. Leading the charge was left-handed pitcher Tarik Skubal. He brought Detroit another Triple Crown winner. He led the AL in wins (18), ERA (2.39), and strikeouts (228). He was the unanimous choice for the AL Cy Young Award. In the playoffs, the Tigers swept the Houston Astros in the AL Wild Card Series. Detroit took a two-games-to-one lead over the Cleveland Guardians in the ALDS. But Cleveland won the next two games to take the series.

As one of the founding franchises of the American League, the Detroit Tigers have contributed generously to MLB history. Tigers fans have rarely had to wait long to root for a contender. With a little luck and a lot of hard work, the Tigers just might rise to the top of the AL jungle again.

Outfielder Riley Greene

INDEX